KU-358-161

This edition first published 1973 by William Collins Sons and Company Limited

© Marshall Cavendish Limited 1971.

Marshall Cavendish Publications Limited 1971

The bulk of the material published in this book was first published by
Marshall Cavendish Limited in "Golden Hands"

Printed in Great Britain

ISBN 0 00 103318 2

LOTS OF FUN TO MAKE A GIFT

Collins · Glasgow and London

STRING HOLDER

KNITTING NEEDLE TIDY

A bag for keeping a ball of string handy

You will need :

Patterned cotton fabric 24 inches by 8 inches wide
Tape for draw string
Pieces of felt or plain fabric for animal shapes
Ball of string
Sewing thread

1. Fold the fabric across the width and sew up the sides to make a bag. Make a 1 inch hem on the upper edge and thread a piece of tape through.
2. Cut out the animal design from felt or fabric and sew to the bag. Plan where the hole will be.
3. Make a hole for the string to come through and buttonhole stitch round the edges of the hole.

Every knitter knows how hard it is to keep knitting needles matched and together. This easy-to-make needle tidy can be made from an odd half-yard of dress or furnishing fabric and makes a pretty present.

You will need :

Patterned fabric 30 inches by 18 inches
$\frac{3}{4}$ yard of 1 inch ribbon
Plain fabric for lining 30 inches by 18 inches

1. Join the two pieces of fabric, right sides facing, on three sides. Turn to the right side and oversew the fourth side closed.
2. Right sides of tidy together, fold up one end to a depth of 8 inches to make a pocket. Pin and tack.
3. Stitch the pocket edges and turn tidy right side out.
4. Mark the pocket into 14 equal divisions, approximately $1\frac{1}{4}$ inches wide, with tacking stitches. Stitch along the tacking lines.
5. Sew two 12 inch lengths of ribbon at each side of the pocket.
6. Fill with needles, roll up and tie the ribbon with a bow.

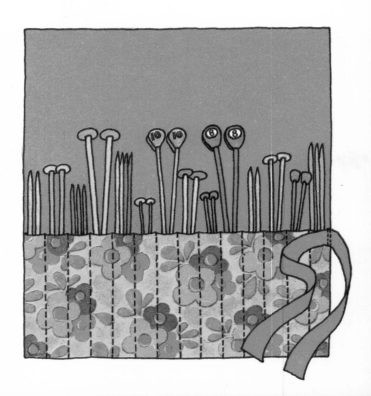

BATH MULES

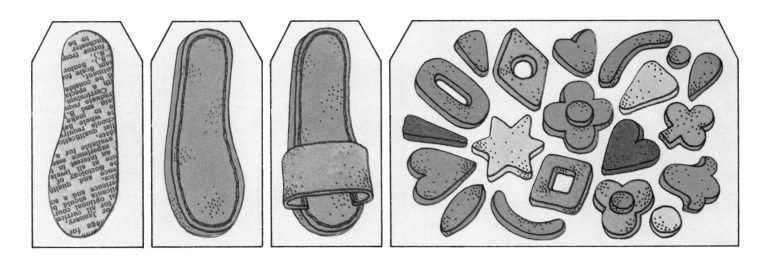

You will need:

- 1 inch thick plastic foam 18 inches by 12 inches for soles
- ¼ inch thick plastic foam 12 inches by 12 inches for uppers and decoration
- Sewing thread

1. Make a paper pattern for the soles by drawing round your own feet. Cut patterns for both left and right feet.
2. Pin patterns to the plastic foam and cut out two sole shapes, adding ½ inch all round.
3. Machine stitch all round both soles ½ inch from the edge, using a large size machine stitch.

4. Cut two strips of the ¼ inch thick plastic foam 3 inches by 6½ inches to make the uppers.
5. Attach each of the uppers to the soles, machine stitching along the previous machining line.
6. Cut the remaining scraps of foam into different shapes —stars, flowers, triangles, squares, crescents, strips or even features to make up amusing faces—and decorate the mule uppers by stitching the shapes on by hand, keeping them very close together. A different kind of decoration can be achieved by cutting holes in the uppers before stitching them to the soles, and adding the cut-out shapes round the holes.

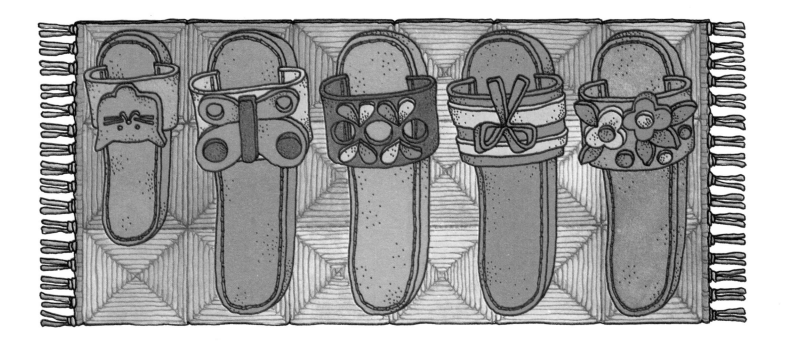

GLOVE PUPPETS

For each puppet allow half a yard of 36 inch wide fabric, plus additional bits of material and wool.

Make a paper pattern from the diagram; one square = one inch.

For the Girl

Cut two main shapes from the fabric.

Cut one circle of pink felt or fabric for the face and sew or stick in position. Sew all round main shapes $\frac{1}{4}$ inch from the edge, leaving the bottom open. Clip the curves and turn to the right side. Hem bottom if necessary. Cut 14 inch long strands of wool and stitch to the middle of the girl's head. Plait the wool either side and tie on ribbons at the bottom. Stitch on pink cheeks, red lips, blue circles for the eyes, draw in eyelashes and fingers with felt marker. Make an apron with ties from a small rectangle of cotton. Add lace edging and lightly tack in position. Make a felt flower and sew to the hand.

The Teddy

Make a basic shape as above, inserting two cut-out felt ears before sewing round. For young children eyes, nose, and inside of ears are better stitched on. Mouth and paws are embroidered, or drawn on with felt marker. The small waistcoat and bow tie are made separately and lightly tacked on.

The Rabbit

Make as above but in fur fabric and with longer ears. Features are stitched or stuck on, whiskers can be pipe cleaners but it is safer to embroider mouth and whiskers. Add bow at neck.

Lion

Use basic shape as above. Knit a few rows of looped stitch for the mane and stitch in place, or sew loops, several rows deep, round the face. A plaited wool tail is sewn on at the back. Features on the face are sewn or stuck on.

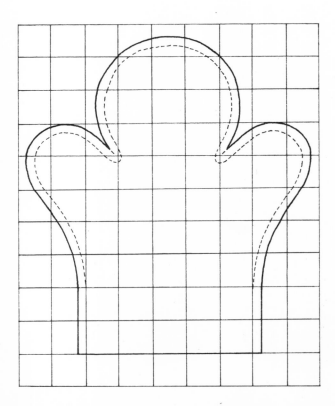

COTTON WOOL BALL HOLDER

You will need:

Net, voile or lace, 18 inches by 18 inches
Fabric for base, velvet, cotton or satin
1 yard narrow lace edging
12 inches narrow velvet ribbon

1. Cut a circle, 7 inches diameter, from base fabric. Cut two similar circles from net.
2. Cut off 7 inches lace edging. Gather remainder and tack round the edge of the base circle, on the right side of the fabric.
3. Take one net circle and mark a line $3\frac{1}{4}$ inches from edge. Cut the small segment off and hem the straight edge. Tack segment in position, matching the curve of the base. Mark and cut second net circle, $2\frac{3}{4}$ inches from edge. Use larger segment. Hem edge and tack segment to base. It will overlap the first segment by $\frac{1}{2}$ inch. Machine stitch all round, through two layers of net, lace and base fabric. Turn holder inside out and press. Trim opening with ribbon and net. Make a ribbon bow for decoration.

LUNCH BAG

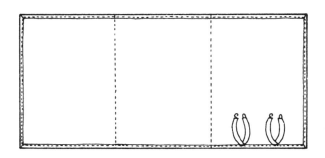

You will need:

36 inches × 18 inches of canvas
2 four-inch lengths elastic
2 hooks and eyes
2 satchel straps
2 leather straps for handles

1. Fold the canvas into 3 even sections.
2. Hem round all edges.
3. On the bottom section 4 inches and 8 inches from the edge, sew the elastic with a hook at each end and an eye to correspond on the inside of the elastic, to make two loops.
4. Sew on satchel straps as shown.
5. Sew on handles.

MAKE A PIN CUSHION

You will need for one pin cushion:

7 inch square of felt
Scraps of felt in different colours
   braid, sequins, etc.
Kapok for stuffing (or better still use dried coffee
   grounds—they prevent the pins from rusting)

Diagrams are 1 square = 1 inch

1. Cut 2 heart shapes, and two lengths 7 inches long ×
1 inch wide. Join the long pieces into a ring. Sew one
heart shape on the top and one on the bottom, leaving
a small opening for stuffing. Sew up when stuffed and
decorate with a small heart and sequins.
2. Cut 2 apple shapes and a pair of leaves and stalk. Sew
up the apples leaving a small opening. Sew on the leaves
and stalk, and then stuff and sew up.
3. Cut 2 shapes and two 7 inch long and 1 inch wide
strips. Sew strips together to form a ring. Sew on the
shapes, one at the bottom and one at the top. Stuff,
sew up. Sew on two circles of braid.
4. Cut 6 2¼ inch squares, sew together into a cube,
stuff, sew up. Sew on braid or edgings.
5. Cut 2 shapes, and 2 strips 5½ inches × 1½ inches, sew
the strips into a ring, stitch in the top and bottom
shapes. Stuff, sew up and decorate with contrasting
circle of felt.
6. Cut 6 segments, stitch together and stuff. Sew up.
Sew on edging down the centre of each segment, and
a bow at the top.

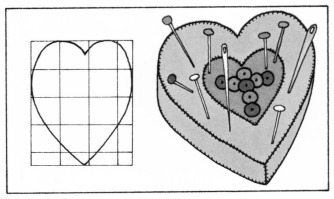

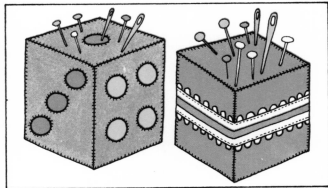

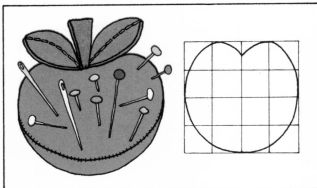

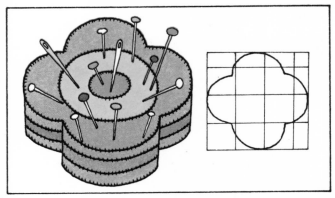

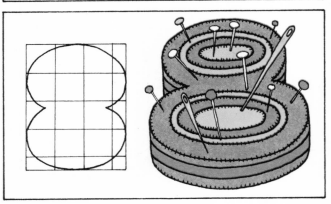

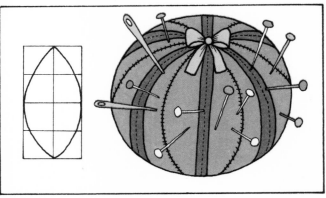

FANCY BELTS

Velvet belts can be made from wide velvet ribbon and petersham.

For plaited belts string is ideal but remember you will need about one third as much again to allow for plaiting. You can also use piping cord, twine or coloured braids. Suede belts require two strips of suede for the length required and need to be stiffened with petersham. To make a beaded belt it is advisable to use invisible plastic thread for strength.

Ideas. Straight plaited belt with a buckle.
Plaited belt with braid tassels at either end.
Canvas belt decorated with satin stitch embroidery.
Straight velvet belt with gold thread design.
Beaded belts of various widths made of strips of bead weaving. Add a buckle.
Suede belt with motifs.
Plain straight belt with tassels to tie at either the front or side.

WRIST PIN CUSHION

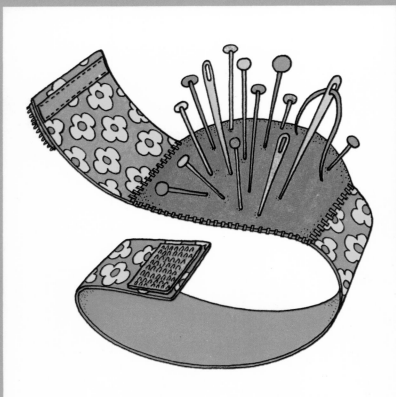

You will need:

Wrist strap fabric 9½ inches × 2½ inches (e.g. velvet, printed cotton, corduroy)

Fabric 9½ inches × 3 inches (e.g. felt or velvet)

Pin cushion felt 2 inches × 2½ inches

Kapok, Terylene filling or bran for padding cushion

Sewing thread

Embroidery thread and/or ribbon 5 inches × ¼ inch wide

Touch and close fastening such as Velcro

2 pieces of thin card 1¾ inches × 2¼ inches

1. Turn the wristband fabric ¼ inch to the wrong side all round, and the lining ⅜ inch. Slip stitch together wrong sides facing (if felt is used for the lining no turnings are needed).

2. Slip stitch the cushion fabric on three sides to form a bubble.

3. Place card between cushion and band and pad firmly with stuffing so that no pins can go through the thickness. Slip stitch the fourth side firmly.

4. Sew touch and close fastening firmly to the ends of the strap to the required length.

PILLAR BOX LINEN BAG

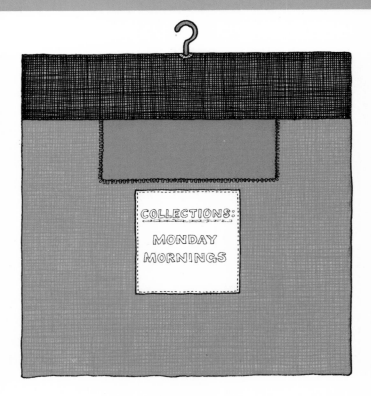

You will need:

Red canvas 36 inches × 18 inches

Black canvas 4 inches × 9 inches

Matching thread

White cotton 4 inches × 6 inches

Coat hanger

Black embroidery thread

1. Make red canvas into a bag by sewing round three edges. Turn out and oversew along fourth edge.

2. 4 inches from the top cut out a piece of fabric 3 inches × 7 inches.

3. Insert coat hanger into this gap.

4. Push coat hanger up to the top of the bag, making a hole in the top for the hook.

5. Oversew round this hole.

6. Oversew round the mouth of the pillar box.

7. Hem black canvas all round.

8. Attach black canvas to top of the bag as shown.

9. Hem all round edges of white cotton.

10. Embroider collecting times on the white cotton.

11. Attach to front of post box.

SEWING KIT

You will need:

Corduroy or velvet 18 inches by 10 inches
Cotton lining fabric 18 inches by 10 inches
Felt for pin book 3 inches by 4 inches
Felt pieces for thimble, measure and scissors holders
Patterned fabric for pocket, 5 inches by 8 inches
Length of shirring elastic
Two decorative buttons
Appliqué motif

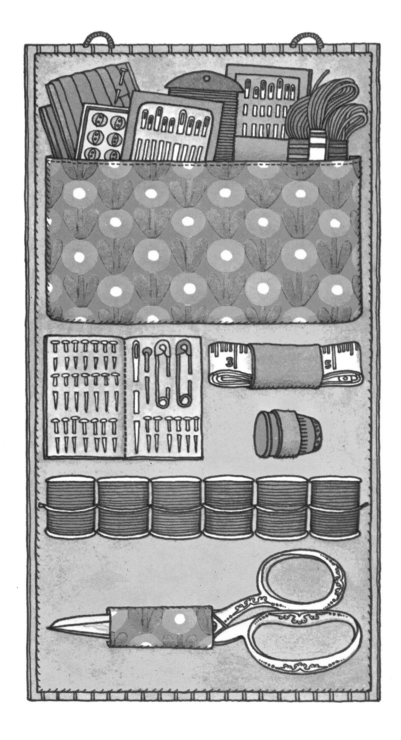

1. Before starting, mark on the cotton lining the position of the pocket, scissors, tape and thimble holders and of the reel elastic. Machine stitch the needle book in position. Neaten the top edge of the pocket, turn in a narrow hem all round and slip stitch in position. Hand sew the felt holders into place. Knot one end of the elastic and thread it into a large-eyed needle. Bring the needle through the lining $\frac{3}{8}$ of an inch from the edge and couch down the elastic firmly at 1 inch intervals, leaving loops large enough to hold the cotton reels.

2. Turn $\frac{1}{2}$ inch hem on all four sides of the corduroy and tack, mitring the corners. Turn hem on all four sides of the lining fabric, tack turnings to the wrong side and position the lining on the corduroy, wrong sides facing, so that a narrow edge of corduroy shows all round.

3. Hand sew the lining to the corduroy with small slip stitches, taking care that the stitches go through the corduroy turnings only and that no stitches show on the outside of the kit. Make two loops on the upper edge. Roll up the kit and sew on two buttons.

POMPOM FUN

You will need:

- Wool
- Card rings
- Scraps of felt
- Small buttons
- Pieces of ribbon

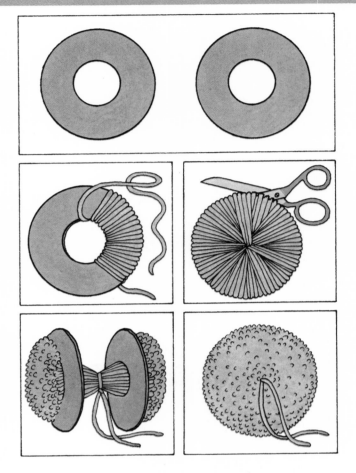

To make a pom-pom, place two card rings together and wind wool round evenly from inside to outside until the centre hole is full. With sharp scissors, cut the wool between the two rings of card, tie the middle tightly with wool and pull off the card rings.

To make a chick you will need one small pom-pom and one large one. Before you remove the card rings from the smaller one, tie in a diamond-shaped piece of felt for the beak. Tie the two pom-poms together by their threads, sew in two small buttons for eyes and stitch on pieces of felt for a pair of feet and a tail. Tie a ribbon round the neck in a bow.

Mouse one very small pom-pom with ears tied in before the rings are removed and one large one with plaited wool tail tied in. Tie the two pom-poms together, sew on feet and buttons for eyes and nose.

Snake fourteen small pom-poms and one larger one with a forked tongue tied in.

Rabbit one large pom-pom for body, one smaller pom-pom for the head with long felt ears tied in, and a small pom-pom for the tail. Sew in button eyes and nose and small felt feet.

BOBBIN RING

BATH-A-BABY APRON

You will need:

1 yard PVC coated cotton fabric
Soft towelling fabric 20 inches by 12 inches
2 yards wide tape, for neck and waist ties
2 curtain rings

1. Make pattern from the graph (1 square = 1 inch). Cut out the apron shape and machine stitch raw edge.
2. Cut towelling 11 inches by 16 inches for the pocket. Stitch top edge and then stitch in position on apron. Cut a heart-shaped piece of towelling, stitch in place for a pin holder. Make a PVC loop to hold curtain rings, stitch loop on apron top left. Make waist ties. Stitch necktie to apron, top right only, fix through curtain rings to fasten and adjust.

You will need:

Light wire (which has been stored in a roll)
Artificial flowers
Metal file
6 inches of satin ribbon
9 full cotton reels
Small tin coloured paint

1. File the end of the wire.
2. Paint the wire.
3. Slide cotton reels onto the loop.
4. Bind two ends of the wire to form a circle.
5. Attach artificial flowers at the top of the circle at the join.
6. Tie ribbon into a loop to hang up.

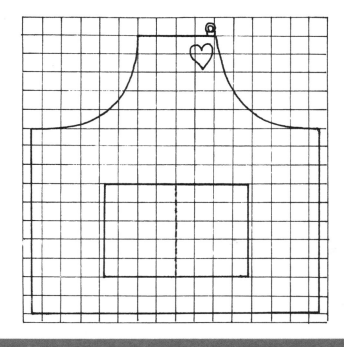

FANCY EDGINGS

These edgings are worked directly onto the fabric by inserting the hook through the weave. A very finely woven lawn can be marked with a row of holes as a guide by running the fabric through an unthreaded sewing machine. To fasten on the cotton, have a slip loop ready in the cotton, insert the hook through the fabric and pull the slip loop through, then work 1 ch to fasten the loop. These edgings may also be worked in a thicker cotton to edge face flannels or guest towels.

You will need

Handkerchiefs with rolled hems
One reel of sewing cotton, or crochet cotton, size 60, 70, 80 or 100
One No. 0.75 (ISK) crochet hook

Hooped edging

Fasten on cotton, 4 ch, leave a space of $\frac{1}{8}$ in, work 1 tr, 7 ch, ss into 3rd of 4 ch at beg, work 9 dc over 7 ch loop, ss to top of last tr, 1 ch, * leave a space of $\frac{1}{8}$ in, 1 tr, 1 ch, leave a space of $\frac{1}{8}$ in, 1 tr, 7 ch, ss into the first of the last 2 tr, work 9 dc over 7 ch loop, ss into last tr, 1 ch, rep from * all round edges of handkerchief, adjusting spacing of tr at corners and ending with ss to 3rd of first 4 ch at beg.

Shell edging

Fasten on cotton, * leave a space equal to the length of a tr and work 7 tr all into the same place to make a shell, work 1 dc at a space equal to the length of a tr from the shell, rep from * all round edges of handkerchief, working a 9 tr shell into each corner. Work last dc into same place as beg.

Picot edging

Fasten on cotton, * 4 ch, work 2 tr into the same place about $\frac{1}{8}$ in from fastening on, 6 ch, ss between the last 2 tr, 4 ch, work 1 dc about $\frac{1}{8}$ in from tr, rep from * all round edges of handkerchief, adjusting spacing at corners as necessary and working last dc into same place as beg.

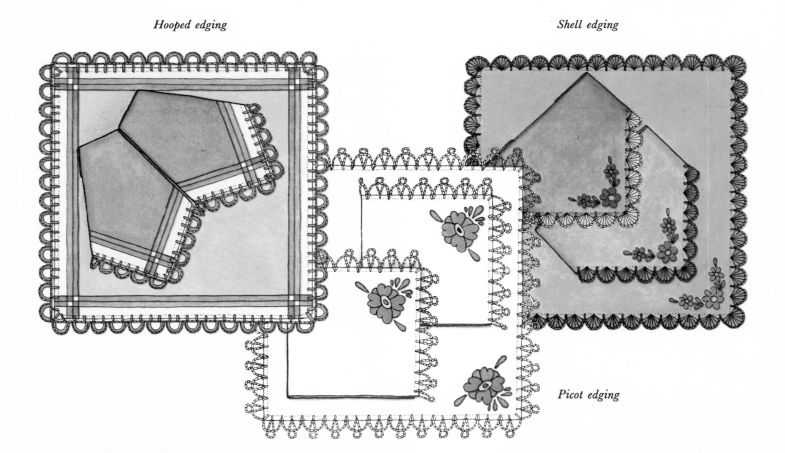

Hooped edging

Shell edging

Picot edging

PRETTY COAT HANGERS

You will need:

Wooden coat hanger
¼ yard 3 ounce weight wadding
Strip of satin or taffeta fabric, 36 inches wide by 4½ inches deep
1 yard contrasting colour ribbon, 1 inch wide
½ yard ribbon of the same colour, ¼ inch wide
Matching threads

1. Cut a strip of wadding across the width of the piece, 2 inches wide, and bind the hanger from end to end, stitching the wadding securely at both ends.
2. Fold the wider ribbon lengthwise and press along the fold.
3. Trim the corners of the strip of satin fabric to round them off.

4. Turn under a ¼ inch hem along both long edges of the strip of satin, including the rounded corners. Tack the folded ribbon under one hem edge so that the ribbon shows ¼ inch. Machine stitch along this hem.
5. Gather both edges of the satin strip to the length of the coat hanger (approximately 18 inches long).
6. Slip the coat hanger inside this casing and hand sew the two edges together along the upper edge of the coat hanger, leaving the contrasting ribbon to stand up like a spine.
7. Bind the hook with the narrow ribbon and secure with one or two stitches.
Make a heart-shaped lavender sachet from the same fabric, edged with contrast ribbon gathers, and hang it from the hook on a loop of ribbon.

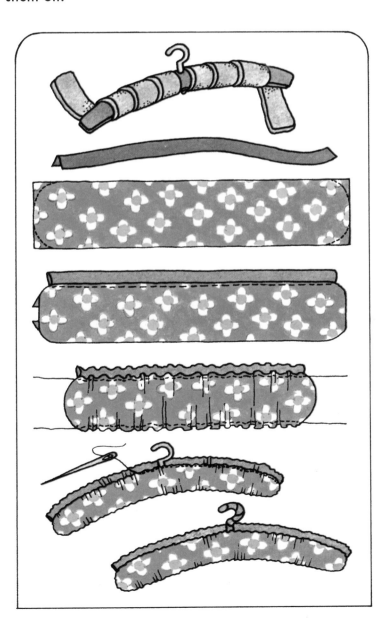

IDEAS FOR TEA TOWELS

Ideas for using tea towels:

1. *Peg bag:* Fold tea towel as shown and sew up both sides. Join up sides of opening about two inches in from each side.

2. *Wall hanging:* Sew tape, wide enough to hold a length of dowling along top of towel at back. Add tassels and cord.

3. *Laundry bag:* Sew two tea towels together along three sides. On inside sew tape leaving ends open. Thread cord or tape through to draw up bag.

4. *Apron:* Turn back two corners, cut and hem. Stitch tape ties at sides and neck. Pocket can be added in contrasting material.

5. *Cushions:* One towel for each cushion. Fold towel in half. Sew up three sides. Insert cushion pad. Add piping or tassels.

FLOWER POT COVER

You will need:

Gardener's raffia, available in hanks
Strong sewing thread

1. Divide the hank into groups of fifteen strands. Knot one end and slip it over a door handle or bureau drawer to anchor the raffia for plaiting.
2. Divide the strands into three groups of five strands and plait very firmly. Knot the end neatly. Make several plaits.
3. Taking one plait, shape it into a round, flat mat, oversewing the edges together. Leave a small hole in the middle to correspond with the drainage hole in the flower pot.
4. Using a flower pot as a guide for size, shape the pot cover by stitching each row of plaiting a fraction further out from the last one. Introduce new plaits by stitching the knots together, leaving the knot on the inside of the pot cover.
5. Continue working round and round until the pot cover is the required depth. Use firm pressure of the fingers to flatten the end of the last plait and fasten off with small stitches on the inside of cover.
6. A matching base mat can be made to stand the flower pot on, using the same method of working as for the pot cover base.

CAR TIDY

Car ashtrays were never designed for toffee papers, lolly sticks and apple cores. The car will look tidier at the end of a journey if a car tidy is used. This one, made of wipe-clean PVC, fastens to the inside of the car door with suction discs.

You will need:

Strip of PVC material, 35 inches long by 8 inches wide; two suction discs; embroidery cotton.

1. Right sides facing, machine stitch the two short edges together.
2. Turn right side out. Fold the double thickness of material to make a pocket 7 inches deep. Ensure that the seam is at the bottom of the pocket, out of sight.
3. Blanket stitch the sides of the pocket closed. Dip the needle in talcum powder to make sewing easier.
4. Using pointed scissors, make two star-shaped holes, I inch down from the upper edge of the tidy, $2\frac{1}{2}$ inches apart.
5. Insert the suction discs.

JEWEL CASE

You will need:

Plate or saucer $6\frac{1}{2}$ inches in diameter
$\frac{1}{2}$ yard of fabric for the cover (satin, heavy silk, velvet, quilted cotton wool)
$\frac{1}{2}$ yard satin for the lining and internal pockets
$1\frac{1}{2}$ yards $\frac{1}{2}$ inch wide braid
Matching thread, tacking cotton
9 inch zip to match cover fabric
Beads or artificial flowers for decoration

1. Using the plate as a template, cut a circle from heavy paper to make the pattern from the top and bottom of the case. For the sides of the case, measure the circumference of the plate and cut a strip of paper to that length plus 1 inch for seam allowance. The strip should be $2\frac{3}{4}$ inches deep.

2. From the cover fabric, using the paper patterns, cut two circles and one strip. Cut two more circles and one strip from the lining fabric. Cut one more strip, twice the length of the paper pattern plus $\frac{1}{4}$ of the overall length, for the inside pockets.

3. Fold the long lining strip in half lengthwise and join the long side. Turn the strip right side out and close the open end. Sew this strip to the right side of the other satin strip as illustrated to make 3 long pockets and 3 small pockets.

Fold the completed strip with pockets in half, pockets side facing and join the short ends. Sew the strip around one of the lining circles.

Sew the second lining circle to the other edge of the strip, leaving a 9 inch opening for the zip.

4. Fold the cover fabric in half and join the short ends. Join the strip to the cover circles, as for the lining, leaving a 9 inch opening for the zip.

5. Place the lining inside the cover, wrong sides facing, so that the openings match. Turn the edges of the opening on the lining and the cover inwards and insert the zip so that the teeth show, but so that the fabric of the zip is hidden. Sew the zip in place by hand. Decorate the top of the case with an artificial flower or beads, or perhaps work an initial on one of the cover circles before assembling the pieces.

OVEN MITT

Make a useful oven mitt with a magnet stitched in so that it can be hung from the cooker.
For one mitt you will need:

¼ yard cotton fabric
18 inches by 36 inches lining material—flannelette, wool or blanketing
Small magnet

1. Make a paper pattern from the chart. Fold the cotton material and cut out two shapes.
2. Using the same pattern, cut out four shapes from the lining material.
3. Sandwich the two cotton shapes, right sides facing, between the four pieces of lining.
4. Machine stitch through the six layers of fabric, ½ inch from the edge, leaving the wrist open.
5. Trim the seam and snip the gusset.
6. Turn right side out and hem the wrist.
7. Cut a strip of cotton for a loop and fold the magnet into the strip.
8. Hand sew the loop to enclose the magnet and stitch the loop to the wrist of the mitt.

Scale: 1 square — 1 inch

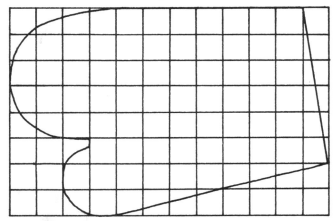

TRIM A BONNET

To make a bonnet, you will need:

½ yard 36 inch wide fabric; ½ yard matching lining; 3 inches narrow elastic

Make pattern from graph (1 square = 1 inch). Cut pieces for main section, back and two ties. Dart back. Gather main section on dotted line to fit back. Make up lining to match and insert into bonnet, turning in ¼ inch turnings. Insert a 3 inch piece elastic into base of neck for close fit. Seam ties and turn inside out. Make crochet trimming.
For the trimming: 2½ inches wide and edging, ⅜ inch wide; 1 ball Coats mercer crochet No. 20, No. 1.25 (ISR) crochet hook.

First strip. 1st row Commence with 5 ch, 1 triple tr (tr̃ tr) into 5th ch from hook, * 10 ch, 1 tr tr into 5th ch from hook, rep from * having one rep from each ¾ inch of required length. Do not turn.
2nd row Into first sp work (3 dc, 5 ch, 3 dc), * 1 dc into each of next 3 ch, (5 ch, 1 ss into last dc), 3 times to make 1 triple picot, 1 dc into each of next 2ch, into next sp work (3 dc, 5 ch, 3dc) * rep from * to * to end of row, 5 ch, do not turn, work along opposite side, into same sp work (3 dc, 5 ch, 3 dc), rep from * to * ending with 2 ch, 1 tr into first dc.
3rd row 1 dc into loop just made, * 11 ch, 1 dc into next 5 ch loop, rep from * all round ending with 11 ch, 1 ss into first dc. Fasten off.

Second strip. Work as first strip for 2 rows.
3rd row 1 dc into loop just made, 11 ch, 1 dc into next 5 ch loop, * 5 ch, 1 ss into corresponding loop on first strip 5 ch, 1 dc into next 5 ch loop on 2nd strip, rep from * along side, 11 ch, 1 dc into next 5 ch loop at end of strip, complete as first strip.
Complete trimming with picot edging on brim and crown.

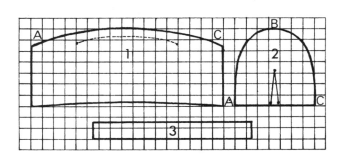

PRETTY PARCELS

1. Make hair for girl and clown of paper strips and stick down. Cut out and glue on features, owl's wings and ears. Tie ribbon round neck. Make a cone of thin card for clown's hat.

2. Decorate plain parcels by sticking on paper shapes, or tie up awkwardly shaped parcels into a cracker.

3. Animal parcels have cut-out features and paws, whiskers of thin card strips, tails of paper, ribbon or cord. Stripes on cat are of ribbon, and the lion's mane is made of looped ribbon.

4. Butterfly and flowers are of crêpe paper, stalks and leaves cut out of coloured paper and stuck down side of box. Wind thin ribbon round outside of candle and stick down a cut-out flame. Make roof for house of thin card and stick on paper windows and door. Attach paper handle to plain box to make a basket parcel. For sun face and television, stick down cut-out paper shapes. Cotton wool, a red button and thin card wafer biscuit make an amusing ice-cream sundae gift-wrapping.

FINGER WEAVING

Finger weaving is an old and primitive technique for making cords, which can be used to make a wide range of fashion and furnishing accessories. Any weight of yarn or thread can be used or mixtures of different kinds of threads. Try leather thongs with velvet ribbon, Lurex ribbon with raffia, chenille yarn with coloured string. Finger-woven cords will vary in thickness depending on the weight of the cord and two cords can be woven together to make an even thicker cord or a wide flat strip. Make hair bows and chignon loops from ribbon cord, shoulder bag straps from woven knitting wool or string, tie belts from raffia or leather. Stitch lengths of finger weaving into unusual place mats or make smart curtain ties. Follow the diagrams below for the techniques.

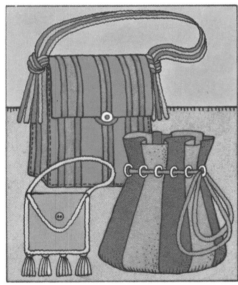

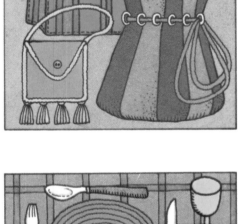

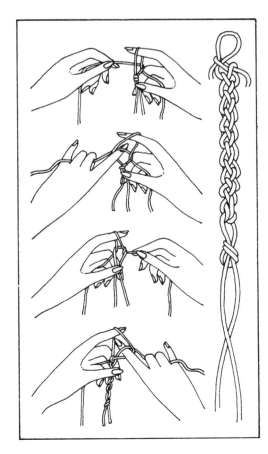

WOOLLY BALL

Bright knitted balls with a tinkling bell inside make attractive presents. The instructions make a ball half white half contrast colour. But by varying the introduction of contrast colour or by bringing in more than one colour, brilliantly striped or panelled balls can be very easily made.

You will need

1 ounce Double knitting yarn, and 1 ounce in contrast colour or oddments to a total of 2 ounces
One pair No. 8 needles
Kapok for stuffing
Small bell
Ball measures 18 inches in circumference

First section

Using No.8 needles and 1st colour cast on 2 sts. K 1 row. Work in garter st, inc one st at each end of next, then following 3rd row twice, then following 4th row twice, then following 6th row twice and following 7th row twice. 20 sts. Work 10 rows without shaping. Break off first colour and join in 2nd colour. Work ten rows without shaping. Decrease one st at each end of next, then following 7th row twice, then following 6th row twice, then following 4th row twice and following 3rd row twice. 2 sts. K 1 row. Cast off. Work 5 more sections in same way using colours as required.

To make up

With right sides facing join side seams of each section leaving about 2 inches of last seam open. Stuff with kapok inserting bell in middle of kapok.
Oversew remaining seam.

Use the trace pattern shape for one segment to make fabric balls. Allow ½ inch turnings all round each segment when cutting out.

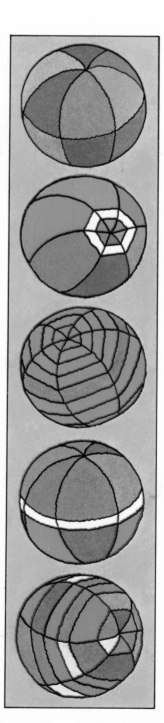

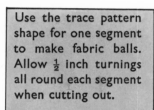

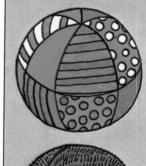

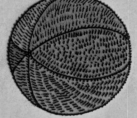

SHOE BAG

You will need:

    24 inches × 36 inches of canvas
    Coathanger
    Sewing thread
    3 strips of cotton 6 inches × 24 inches

1. Hem round three edges of the canvas.
2. Fold over 1½ inches on the top edge of canvas, insert coat hanger, and hem along edge.
3. Hem all round the three strips of cotton.
4. Sew to canvas, starting at the bottom, leaving 6 inches between each strip.
5. Sew through cotton and canvas at 3 inch intervals to form pockets.

Note—for a shoe polish tidy or sewing tidy simply buy small quantities of canvas and cotton and make smaller pockets.

POMANDERS

You will need:

    1 orange
    12 inches of ribbon
    2 plastic-headed pins
    Box of cloves

1. Tie ribbon or braid round orange in the middle securing at top and bottom with pin.
2. Leave a loop at the top with which to hang pomander.
3. Stick cloves into skin of orange and cover the fruit completely.
4. Hang in wardrobe.

Half-completed orange showing space for ribbon drawn on by felt pen.

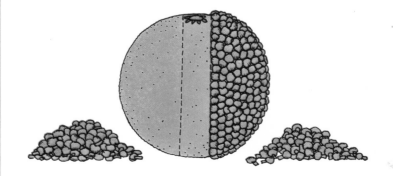

MOB CAP

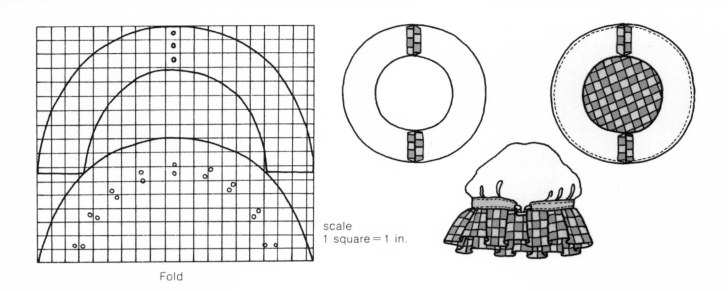

scale
1 square = 1 in.

Fold

Make a pretty mob cap to wear as a bath hat or for a charming bonnet to match a dress.

You will need:

- ¾ yard 36 inch fabric (any kind, but plastic for a bath hat)
- 1½ yards 1 inch wide tape
- ½ inch wide elastic

1. Make a pattern for crown and brim pieces, copying the graph onto 1 inch squared paper. Pin the pattern pieces onto the fabric, the crown lying along the fold as shown in the diagram. Cut out (three pieces).

2. Seam the two brim pieces to make a ring. Place the brim section on the crown section, right sides facing, and stitch them together as shown. Turn the cap right sides out and then fold the brim back on itself, wrong sides together, thus making a doubled fabric brim, the raw edge lying along the seam. Press.

3. Stitch the casing tape on the inside of the cap, to cover the seam as shown, leaving an opening for inserting the elastic. Cut a piece of elastic to fit the head when stretched. Insert. Join ends. Trim as required.

TISSUE-BOX COVER

To cover a large box of tissues, you will need:

$\frac{1}{2}$ yard of 36 inch wide fabric, any remnant will do. $\frac{5}{8}$ yard of $\frac{1}{4}$ inch wide elastic

Trimmings: lace edging, cord, braid or artificial flowers

1. Cut a paper pattern from the chart. Pin the pattern to the fabric and cut out the shape twice.

2. Right sides facing, machine stitch between points A-a and b-B, leaving a-b open. Fold the seam edges a-b to the wrong side and press.

3. On the wrong side, stitch the corner seams, marked on the chart in blue. Press the seams open and trim.

4. Make a $\frac{1}{2}$ inch hem along all four edges, leaving a $\frac{1}{2}$ inch opening. This is the casing for the elastic.

5. Trim the box cover after it has been stitched but before the elastic is inserted.

6. Thread the elastic through the opening and adjust to fit the tissue box, overlapping the ends of the elastic $\frac{1}{2}$ inch. Stitch the ends securely and close the casing opening.

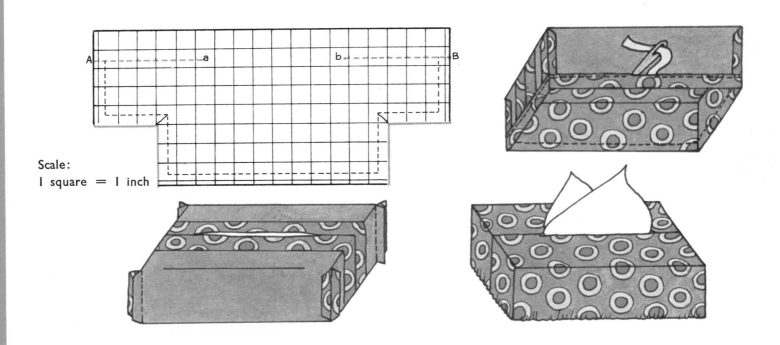

Scale:
1 square = 1 inch

HOW TO STENCIL

You will need:

Stiff card, not too thick. A sharp knife e.g. Stanley knife. Spray paint in cans/oil bound, enamel, or poster paint. Square-ended brush made of stiff bristles.

Choose a motif that is versatile and can be used singly or in repeat. Cut out shapes from card with your sharp knife, leaving a bridge of card between shapes (as in flower). The edges must be clean-cut. Place the card on the object to be stencilled (on round or curved objects fix in position with sticky tape). If you are using a can of spray paint, follow the instructions carefully. Remove the stencil carefully without smudging.

If you want to stencil with a brush you get a softer effect if you keep the poster paint thick and smooth, the oil paint bound, or the enamel lump-free, and use very sparingly on the brush. Stipple it on through the stencil right over the edges with short stabbing movements. Repeat as many times as you want allowing the shapes to dry if the stencil is to overlap, or if using more than one colour.

Suggested use for stencil work: book covers, tins, boxes, coat hangers, toys, lampshades, mats, back of hair brush, mirror.

COLOURFUL CUSHIONS

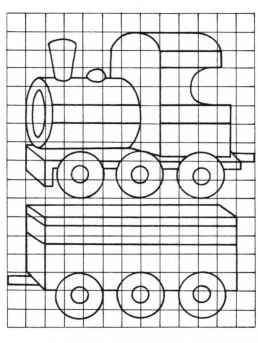

You will need:

1¼ yards of 36 inch wide fabric
Thread
Felt or other non-fraying material
Stuffing

1. Cut out 6 pieces of material each 14 inches square.
2. Cut out appliqué train from felt.
3. Stitch the appliqué train to the right side of three pieces of material.
4. Right sides facing, hem round the edges leaving a small gap at one side.
5. Turn inside out.
6. Stuff the cushion.
7. Blind stitch the gap together.

BUTTON MAGIC

You will need:

> A collection of buttons
> Thick felt or fabric
> Strong thread (polyester)

For the mats cut out the shapes from the felt or fabric. Draw round a dinner plate for circular table mats, for other shapes cut a template from newspaper and draw round it onto the felt.

Sew on buttons in a regular pattern, selecting them for colour and texture. The finished mats could be stuck onto cork, thin card or polystyrene tiles and trimmed. *For the pictures* keep the subject matter simple, so that you can have fun with the textures and shapes of the buttons. Build up the picture section by section, perhaps using contrasting thread in some places. Mount onto heavy card or thin wood. Paint the edges black and attach picture frame rings on the back to hang them up.

CANVAS TOTE-BAG

SPARKLING DECORATIONS

You will need:

Lightweight canvas 24 inches by 36 inches
Button twist thread
Fabric adhesive; button or snap fastener

1. Cut canvas into pieces as follows: 1 piece 36 inches by 12 inches (front, base, back, A), 2 pieces 15 inches by 6 inches (side gussets, B), 1 piece 6 inches by 4 inches (flap fastening, C), 2 pieces 12 inches by 2 inches (handles, D).
2. Turn in short ends piece A ½ inch. Glue down firmly. Turn in ½ inch one short end piece B. Glue firmly. Fold in all raw edges pieces A and B ¼ inch and glue firmly. Seam gussets into bag, wrong sides facing. Top-stitch.
3. Turn in edges piece C. Glue, then top-stitch. Stitch to one edge of bag opening.
4. Fold pieces D lengthwise, turn in raw edges ¼ inch, glue and top-stitch. Stitch to bag. Add button and loop or stud fastening. Decorate with appliqué or bright braid.

A beautiful collection of hanging ornaments are made using scraps of felt embroidered with bright silks and decorated with sequins, glass beads and glittering braids. Plan each decoration to be about 2-2½ inches deep when it is completed.

Cut out the number of felt pieces required for each ornament: cubes, for instance, will require six squares of felt: a star shape is made from four star-shaped pieces; a cone needs three pieces and a base; and a ball requires six segments. Work all the surface embroidery before piecing together, and use kapok for stuffing the ornaments. Stitch beads and sequins on after stuffing. Make bead and wire loops.

LAVENDER BAGS

PICNIC BASKET

You will need:

Lavender
Scraps of material
Ribbons
Bows

1. Fold material and cut out the shape required on the doubled material.
2. Place the right sides together and hem round the edge leaving a small gap at one end so that the bag can be turned inside out.
3. Turn inside out so that the right sides are now on the outside.
4. Fill the bag with lavender through the gap left in the stitching.
5. Blind stitch the gap together.
6. Bows and ribbons can be sewn on as required.

Bottom left: Take a freshly picked bunch of lavender, tie below flower heads, turn stalks outwards and upwards enclosing flower heads. Tie ends with ribbon and trim off uneven stalks.

You will need:

Cane or plastic basket
48 inch wide cotton fabric
$1\frac{1}{4}$ yards narrow cord

1. Measure the width of the basket bottom. Add to this measurement the depth of the basket, plus 12 inches. Cut a piece of fabric 48 inches wide by your total measurement.
2. Join the sides, making a $\frac{1}{2}$ inch seam. Make a $\frac{3}{4}$ inch casing to take the cord along the upper edge. Gather up the lower edge with two rows of gathering, stitching $\frac{1}{4}$ inch and $\frac{3}{8}$ inch from the raw edge.
3. Place the 'bag' inside the basket so that the gathered end lies on the bottom. Hand-stitch the fabric lining to the basket, using double thread, and stitching through the basket just under the rim. Thread the cord through the casing, draw up and tie the ends.

DOLL'S BED

A doll's bed tidy for five dolls, which can be hung alongside a little girl's bed.

You will need:

  Hessian or similar heavy fabric for the background, 36 inches by 18 inches
  Cotton fabric for the bed sheet 36 inches by 27 inches
  Patterned fabric for the coverlet 36 inches by 12 inches
  Cotton wool padding for the pillow. 2⅔ yards lace edging
  42 inches of wood dowelling 1 inch diameter and 2 beads
  Thick cotton cord

1. Tack a ½ inch hem to the wrong side on three sides of the hessian. On the fourth, long side, turn a 1½ inch hem and machine stitch to make a channel (the rod will go through this channel when the tidy is completed). Mark with tacking stitches a line ½ inch below the stitched line from points A-B. Mark another tacking line 8 inches down from A-B to mark points E and F. Tack the cotton wool in place.

2. Tack a narrow hem to the wrong side of the bed sheet fabric on all four sides. Stitch a piece of lace edging along one of the long sides for the sheet turn-down. Tack the sheet to the hessian backing, wrong side of sheet to right side of hessian matching A-a, B-b, C-c, D-d. Fold the sheet up to make a pocket matching g-E and h-F. The lace edge lies free.

3. Cut the coverlet fabric and make a tacked hem to the wrong side on all four sides. Tuck the coverlet under the turned down sheet, matching all four corners, g, h, c, d. Tack the coverlet in place and then machine stitch all round the bed tidy, ¼ inch from the edge, along the line A-B-F-D-E-A through hessian, sheet and coverlet.

4. Tack vertically through the coverlet, sheet and hessian backing at 7 inch intervals to make five pockets. Machine stitch along the tacking lines, matching sewing thread to the sheeting. Hand sew lace edging to outline each pillow.

5. Push the dowelling rod through the channel and slip a large wooden bead onto each end. Knot the cotton cord to each end of the rod to hang the bed tidy from a hook.

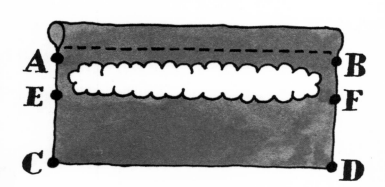

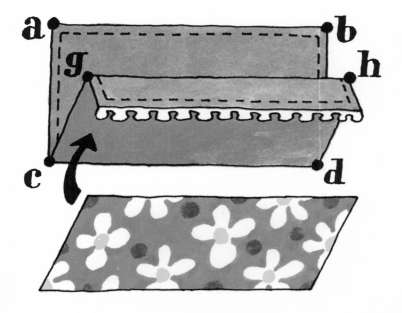

NURSERY HOLD-ALL

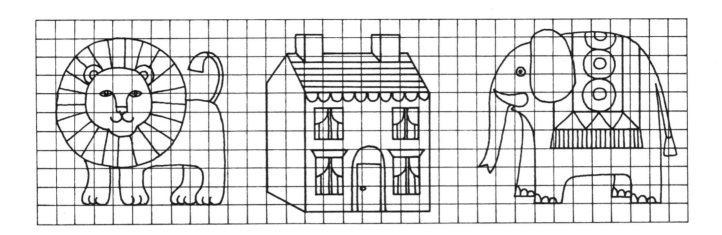

You will need:

1 yard of 36 inch strong fabric
1 yard of 36 inch lining in contrasting colour thread
Motifs of felt material

1. Cut out motifs.
2. Sew motifs onto the fabric at three regular intervals as shown in diagram.
3. With right sides of both pieces of material (fabric and lining) facing, hem round edges leaving a small gap.
4. Turn inside out.
5. Stitch the gap together so that the stitching does not show.
6. Fold the material linings together as shown in the illustration.
7. Sew fabric to fabric to form pockets at three regular intervals (about 1 inch each).
8. Sew on loops and hang.

LUGGAGE LABELS

For a set of six labels you will need:

Odd pieces of brightly coloured leather with two pieces measuring 5 inches by 3½ inches for the large trunk labels.

Sheet of acetate film; six small buckles; white card; matching sewing thread. Make the large trunk labels first: the instructions for the smaller labels are the same.

1. On one of the larger pieces of leather, draw and then cut out (using a razor blade) a hole measuring 2¼ inches deep by 3⅞ inches wide. Cut a piece of acetate film slightly larger than the hole and place it between the two pieces of leather, wrong sides facing. Machine stitch, using a large

stitch, ⅜ inch from the outer edge, leaving one end open for inserting the address card. Cut the corners off diagonally.

2. Cut a slot through both thicknesses of leather about ¾ inch long, ¼ inch from the open end (the slot will be shorter on the smaller labels). Cut a strap 6 inches long by 1 inch wide and stitch the buckle to one end. Point the other.

3. Cut a piece of card 2½ inches deep by 4¼ inches wide and insert it under the acetate film. Thread the strap through the slots and fasten the buckle. The shapes of the other labels can be varied—they can be round, heart-shaped, or oblong. Pack a set of six together for an attractive present.

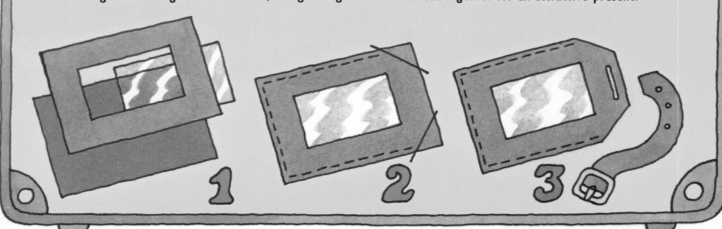